T0379573

DOLLY PARTON

THIS EDITION

Produced for DK by WonderLab Group LLC
Jennifer Emmett, Erica Green, Kate Hale, *Founders*

Editor Maya Myers; **Photography Editor** Kelley Miller; **Managing Editor** Rachel Houghton;
Designers Project Design Company; **Researcher** Michelle Harris; **Copy Editor** Lori Merritt;
Indexer Connie Binder; **Proofreader** Susan K. Hom; **Series Reading Specialist** Dr. Jennifer Albro

First American Edition, 2025
Published in the United States by DK Publishing, a division of Penguin Random House LLC
1745 Broadway, 20th Floor, New York, NY 10019

A catalog record for this book is available from the Library of Congress.
HC ISBN: 978-0-5939-6623-5
PB ISBN: 978-0-5939-6622-8

DK books are available at special discounts when purchased in bulk for sales promotions, premiums, fund-raising, or educational use.
For details, contact:
DK Publishing Special Markets, 1745 Broadway, 20th Floor, New York, NY 10019
SpecialSales@dk.com

Printed and bound in China
Super Readers Lexile® levels 800L to 1010L
Lexile® is the registered trademark of MetaMetrics, Inc. Copyright © 2024 MetaMetrics, Inc. All rights reserved.

The publisher would like to thank the following for their kind permission to reproduce their images:
a=above; c=center; b=below; l=left; r=right; t=top; b/g=background
Alamy Stock Photo: AFF / Curtis Hilbun 1, 48-49t, 52, AFF / Curtis Hilburn 15, AFF / Tammie Arroyo 49tr, Allen Brown 44-45b, Ron Buskirk 43b,
Steve Cukrov 53b, Gina Kelly 11t, John Barrett / PHOTOlink / MediaPunch 38t, MediaPunch Inc 10tl, Pa Images / Bob Collier 54tl, Gavin Rodgers /
Pixel8000 51, Prestor Pictures LLC 26br, Records 33cl, 33cb, Stephen Saks Photography 44tl, © TriStar Pictures / Courtesy Everett Collection 39l,
© Tammie Arroyo / AFF-USA.com 57c; **Bear Family Records:** 23tr; **Courtesy of Imagination Library:** 54-55b, 56tl; **Dreamstime.com:**
Aprescindere 50br, Bombaert 21tr, Daveallenphoto 32ca, Empire331 49crb, Sandamali Fernando 40tl, Sandra Foyt 7b, Natalia Kostikova 55cra,
Littleny 6-7, Theo Malings 10br, Oleksandra Martsinkevich 11b, Boris Medvedev 32br, M.e. Mulder 14, Rolf52 16-17t, Sdbower 32tl, Pavlo Syvak 29cra,
Sorapop Udomsri 19bl, 21cl, 37bl, 52br, 55crb, 59bl, 61cr, Yifang Zhao 49br; **Getty Images:** Archive Photos / Blank Archives 17bl, Archive Photos /
Hulton Archive / Stringer 17tr, Archive Photos / Paul Natkin 33tl, 41cl, Archive Photos / Ron Davis 43t, David Becker / Stringer 35br, Bettmann 18,
30tl, Jon Morgan / CBS 57bl, 57br, © Wally Mcnamee / Corbis 47tr, Found Image Holdings / Corbis 20-21, Henry Diltz / Corbis 47l, Steve Schapiro /
Corbis 31tr, Donaldson Collection / Michael Ochs Archives 33cra, 33cr, Donaldson Collection / Michael Ochs Archives / Stringer 32cl, Michael
Loccisano / FilmMagic for Country Music Association / Staff 50, Shannon Finney 26tl, Erika Goldring / Stringer 53t, Michael Ochs Archives / Stringer
9b, 20cl, 24tl, 24-25, 27, 33bl, 52br, 55crb, 59bl, Richard McCaffrey / Michael Ochs Archive 4-5, Moviepix / 20th Century Fox / Handout 38b,
Peter Kramer / Staff 41bl, Pool 58-59t, Beth Gwinn / Redferns 46, GAB Archive / Redferns 12tl, Pete Still / Redferns 3, Jim Smeal / Ron Galella
Collection 48cla, Ron Galella, Ltd. / Ron Galella Collection 42, John Seakwood / Disney General Entertainment Content / © ABC 8tl, 8-9t,
Craig Sjodin / Walt Disney Television / Disney General Entertainment Content / © ABC 30-31b, Jim Wilkes / Toronto Star 25br, Jeffrey Greenberg /
Universal Images Group 55tr, Kevin Winter / Staff 59tr, Chris Walter / WireImage 39tr; **Getty Images / iStock:** DigitalVision Vectors / traffic_
analyzer 40-41b, hydrangea100 22-23b, Philartphace 19crca, Selektor 49bl, tota 32-33, WerksMedia 61tl; **Grand Ole Opry Archives:** 22;
IMAGN: © Eileen Blass-USA TODAY NETWORK v 56bl, © News Sentinel-USA TODAY NETWORK 36tl; **Penguin Random House:** 56tl;
Shutterstock.com: 20th Century Fox / Kobal 36bl, 36-37b, AFF-USA 44bl, 61, Barr / Mediapunch 29tl, Bei 41tl, Blueee77 37cra, Melissa Herzog
45crb, ITV 34-35t, Gwinn / Mediapunch 32bl, Nancy Barr / Mediapunch 10cr, Nancy Barr Brandon / MediaPunch 10bc, 11c, 12-13b, 19,
John Salangsang 61bl, Donald R Slaughter 45bc, Snap 28

Cover images: Front: **Alamy Stock Photo:** Emma Stoner b; **Dreamstime.com:** Alexaldo; **Getty Images / iStock:** surachetkhamsuk cla;
Back: **Dreamstime.com:** Tartilastock clb; **Shutterstock.com:** tynyuk cra

www.dk.com

DOLLY PARTON

Becky Baines

CONTENTS

MY TENNESSEE MOUNTAIN HOME

If you take a trip to east Tennessee, you'll find all kinds of fun things to do. People travel from all over to visit the theme parks, restaurants, cabins, and museums. They're all near a small town called Sevierville, nestled in the foothills of the Great Smoky Mountains.

Mighty Mountains
The Great Smoky Mountains are part of the Appalachian Mountain range, some of the oldest mountains on Earth. They cover part of 13 states and span over 206,000 square miles (533,538 sq km). They have been around since the time of the dinosaurs!

A once-sleepy mountain town might be the last place you'd expect to find a busy theme park—but there's a very good reason. It's the hometown of Dolly Parton!

Dolly at her family's cabin

Momma and Daddy Robert Parton and Avie Lee Owens met and married in 1939. She was a preacher's daughter from North Carolina. He was a farm boy, born and raised in Tennessee.

Dolly Rebecca Parton was born in Locust Ridge, Tennessee, in 1946. The fourth of 12 kids, Dolly shared a one-bedroom log cabin with her father, mother, and siblings.

Dolly's parents worked hard. Her mother had her hands full looking after 12 children! They may not have had much space, but they had a lot of love.

Special Bond
When Dolly was nine, her mother gave birth to her ninth child, Larry. Dolly felt a special connection with her brother. Her mother called him "Dolly's baby." She even woke up in the night to rock him to sleep when he cried. Sadly, Larry died at just four days old. Dolly said this sad memory helped shape who she is.

Dolly's father was a sharecropper. He rented land to grow tobacco crops. He also worked in construction. Dolly's family was very poor. But they always joked that they never knew it "till some smart aleck" told them!

Dolly, age 9

The Partons' tiny cabin on the mountain had no running water or electricity. In the summertime, Dolly and her brothers and sisters would catch fireflies in jars to help light the room.

A Whole Lotta Love
Dolly's favorite Christmas was the one when her dad bought her mom a wedding ring. Avie Lee had never had one, and Robert decided it was about time. There would be no money for other gifts, but Dolly and her siblings didn't care. They were just happy to see their mom so happy.

Dolly and her family in 1951 (above) and Dolly at age 5 (left)

Replica of the family's cabin at Dollywood

Tennessee Mountain Home

THESE MOUNTAINS AND MY CHILDHOOD HOME HAVE A SPECIAL PLACE IN MY HEART. THEY INSPIRE MY MUSIC AND MY LIFE. I HOPE BEING HERE DOES THE SAME FOR YOU! *Dolly*

Dolly in 1949

The family couldn't afford to spend money on entertainment. Instead, they would pass the time with music. Dolly liked to play makeshift musical instruments and sing to the chickens and the pigs and whoever would listen.

Time Travel

As a tribute to her mother, Dolly constructed an exact copy of her childhood home at her Dollywood theme park in Pigeon Forge, Tennessee. The cabin was built by Dolly's brother Bobby, and Avie Lee designed the inside. It contains many mementos from Dolly's childhood. It's like taking a trip to the 1950s!

Some say that success takes a lot of hard work and a little bit of luck. Dolly learned about hard work from her parents. And she was lucky to be born into a very talented family!

Jake Owens

Dolly's family, 1961

Dolly's grandfather, Jake Owens, was a preacher. He played the fiddle, sang, and wrote church music, including a song recorded by Kitty Wells. His daughter, Avie Lee, shared the family's musical talent with her children.

Dolly

Country Music
The roots of country music go back to the 1700s. Immigrants from Europe and enslaved people from Africa brought folk songs and ballads from their home countries to America. These sounds blended with hymns and work songs that focused on the hardships of every day life. It wasn't just music, it was storytelling. As Americans headed west on the new frontier, they took only instruments they could carry, such as guitars and banjos. What started out of necessity became country's signature sound.

MAKING A NAME

When she was seven, Dolly made her first guitar out of a mandolin and two guitar strings. The next year, her uncle Bill gifted her the real deal: an "itsy-bitsy" Martin guitar. Dolly treasured it.

Of all the people who helped Dolly fall in love with music, Uncle Bill was the one who put her on the road to stardom. He saw Dolly's potential when she was very young. He got her a spot on a local radio program.

When she was 10, Dolly performed on a radio show called *The Cas Walker Farm and Home Hour*. The studio audience fell in love with her big voice. She became a regular and came back to sing on the show even after fame came calling.

Uncle Bill and Dolly in 2011

Uncle Bill
Bill Owens was a singer and songwriter. After Dolly got her start on the radio, he also helped her get on TV. He and Dolly co-wrote the song "Put It Off Until Tomorrow," as well as songs for other famous artists.

The Ryman Auditorium

The Grand Ole Opry

The Grand Ole Opry has been the main stage for country music for a hundred years. A live radio show has been broadcast from this Nashville stage since 1925. Countless music legends have performed at the Opry. The location has changed, but you can still see performances at both the new and original location (now called the Ryman Auditorium).

By 1959, Dolly was a local celebrity. At just 13 years old, she was asked to sing on country music's biggest stage: the Grand Ole Opry. Uncle Bill and his friends had convinced a regular on the show to give one of his Saturday night spots to Dolly. She was introduced by country music legend Johnny Cash.

The Man in Black

Johnny Cash (1932–2003) was famous for his simple style, deep voice, and meaningful messages. He preferred to wear black. He sang about the hardships everyday people faced.

Dolly sang the country hit "You Gotta Be My Baby." The crowd cheered so loud she performed three encores.

SOUVENIR PROGRAM

THE GRAND OLE OPRY

THE MOTHER CHURCH OF COUNTRY MUSIC

Dolly became very popular on local stages and radio. Soon, she had her first record deal. In 1962, Uncle Bill took her to Nashville, Tennessee. She recorded "It's Sure Gonna Hurt." But the record failed to make the music charts. Dolly was dropped by her recording studio. She headed back home.

But she continued recording for a smaller label for the next two years. And when she graduated high school, she was off to Nashville again—for good this time!

The Fisk Jubilee Singers around 1880

18

Dolly at age 14

The Flip Side
A single record had an A-side and a B-side. A popular song was featured on the A-side. A different song was on the back, or B-side.

"The way I see it, if you want the rainbow, you gotta put up with the rain."

Dolly was outside the Wishy Washy laundromat in Nashville in 1964 when a man approached her. He said he was concerned that she was going to get a sunburn. His name was Carl Dean. Two years later, Dolly and Carl would be married. They're still married today.

Dolly in 1965

Dolly was more determined than ever to make it as a singer. In 1965, she signed a contract with famous Monument Records. She spent the next year writing music, recording, and playing live venues around Nashville.

"You'll never do a whole lot unless you're brave enough to try."

Dolly singing on *The Porter Wagoner Show*, 1967

Not-So-Dumb Blonde

Throughout her career, Dolly Parton has been breaking molds and shattering stereotypes. She demands people take her seriously as a musician and businesswoman. And she stays true to herself and the look she loves. She wears her hair as big and blond as possible, and her nails long and red. Her outfits often shimmer with rhinestones.

In 1966, a singer named Bill Phillips wanted to record the song Dolly had written with Uncle Bill. And he wanted "the girl on the demo" to sing it with him. Dolly lent her voice to the background, and people took notice. Finally, in 1967, her song "Dumb Blonde" became the #24 country song in the nation. Then, "Something Fishy" made it to #17. Overnight, everyone was talking about the new singer with the big voice and even bigger hair.

Later that year, she released her first full album, *Hello, I'm Dolly*. The album had 12 songs. And it caught the attention of someone who would help change the course of her career.

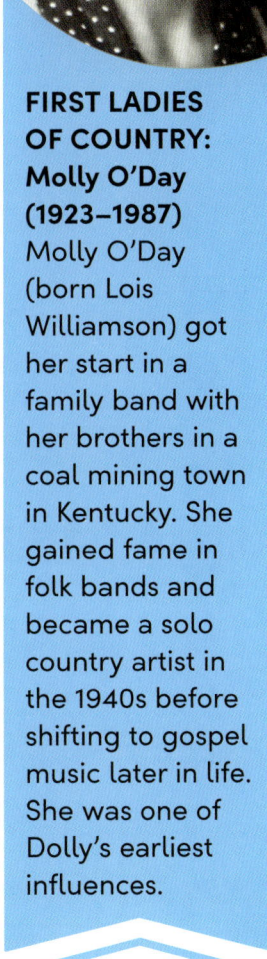

FIRST LADIES OF COUNTRY: Molly O'Day (1923–1987) Molly O'Day (born Lois Williamson) got her start in a family band with her brothers in a coal mining town in Kentucky. She gained fame in folk bands and became a solo country artist in the 1940s before shifting to gospel music later in life. She was one of Dolly's earliest influences.

BIG BREAK

Porter Wagoner was a star of the Grand Ole Opry in the 1950s. He got his own TV show in 1960. He was known for his flashy suits, his wacky sense of humor, and his country twang. Audiences loved him! *The Porter Wagoner Show* ran for 20 years. It featured famous bands, comedians, and up-and-coming singers.

Birds of a Feather
Dolly often said, "Keep your dreams big and your hair bigger." When she met Porter Wagoner, she said she could "relate to his shiny bright costumes, his flashy smile, and his blond helmet."

In 1967, Porter was looking for a new duet partner. He invited Dolly to appear on his show. Their showy outfits and complementary voices made them quite a pair! The crowd went wild. She became his regular performing partner. Together, they created 14 #1 hits.

Dolly and Porter performing together around 1967

Double Take
Dolly once entered a Dolly Parton look-alike contest—and lost! The winner was decided by audience applause. Keeping her identity secret, she paraded across the stage, earning the least applause of anyone there! She found this very funny.

A Dolly Parton impersonator

Keep the Receipt

Dolly's favorite song she's ever written is 1971's "Coat of Many Colors." It's about the pride she felt wearing the beautiful coat her mother sewed from rags when Dolly was a little girl—a coat her classmates made fun of. When the lyrics popped into her head, she wrote them on Porter's dry-cleaning receipt. When the song became a top-five country hit, he had it framed.

Dolly was a hit with TV audiences. Porter's show quickly became the most-watched TV program across the country. Porter and Dolly were signed as a duo to a new label: RCA Records. In 1968, the pair won the Country Music Association (CMA) Award for Vocal Group of the Year.

Dolly was also signed by RCA as a solo artist. In 1971, she had her first #1 solo hit, "Joshua."

Together, Porter and Dolly enjoyed seven years of success together on TV and in the studio.

Porter and Dolly with their band, the Wagonmasters, around 1968

I Will Always Love You

I Will Always Love You

Dolly's song "I Will Always Love You" was her goodbye letter to Porter Wagoner. He called it the most beautiful song he had ever heard. It became so popular that Elvis Presley wanted to record it. But Dolly found out she would have to give him half of the publishing rights. Every time the song was played anywhere, recorded by anyone (including Dolly herself), or included in any movie or TV show, Elvis would receive half the money. Dolly couldn't agree to this.

By 1974, Dolly's career was unstoppable. Her song "Jolene" soared to #1 on the country charts. It even appeared on the pop charts. Her next four releases, including "I Will Always Love You," all hit #1 as well. Only one was a duet with Porter.

Dolly's star was rising while Porter's was slipping. She was ready for a new adventure, but he wasn't ready to let go of their partnership. The two exchanged angry words. Dolly wrote Porter a song to explain how she felt. They parted ways.

Elvis Presley

Dolly performing in 1970

Chart-Toppers
Every genre of music has its own weekly ranking, or chart. Being on more than one chart means a bigger audience. If lovers of country and lovers of pop both liked Dolly's music, that meant more listeners and more album sales.

Later, Porter would take her to court, saying she did not fulfill her contract with him. But they eventually made up. They even made another duet album in 1980.

HELLO, DOLLY!

Dolly Parton was the biggest name in country music. She won the CMA for Female Vocalist of the Year in both 1975 and 1976. Later that year, she hosted her own TV show called *Dolly!* She sang her hits, and she had a guest act for each episode.

Big and Bold
Dolly! was the most expensive show of its time. Each episode cost nearly $100,000 to produce—over half a million dollars today.

Dolly is one of a few stars who can be recognized by her first name alone.

The show was a huge success, quickly becoming the most-watched show in America. But the long days and heavy workload were exhausting. After 26 episodes, she was done.

Dolly with Little Richard on the *Dolly!* reboot in 1987

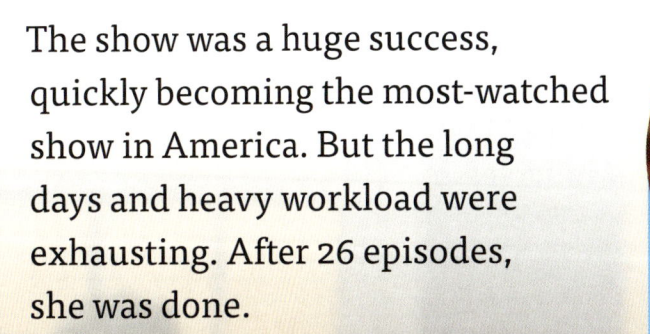

FIRST LADIES OF COUNTRY: Loretta Lynn (1932–2022) Like Dolly, Loretta Lynn grew up very poor in a one-bedroom cabin. But with a $17 guitar, she found fame beyond her wildest dreams. People were drawn to her beautiful voice and flair for storytelling. A book and film about her life, both titled *Coal Miner's Daughter*, became hits in the 1980s.

Many people consider the albums Dolly released in the 1970s the most important of her career. They were so successful that they became a soundtrack for the entire decade!

1971: *Joshua* Title song was her first to go #1

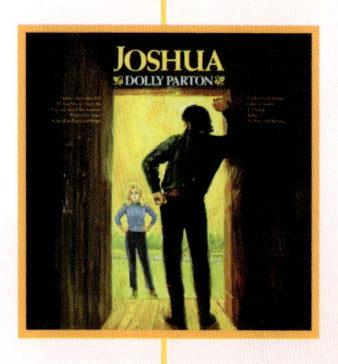

1973: *My Tennessee Mountain Home* Songs about her childhood, often considered Dolly's best album

1971: *Coat of Many Colors* Named one of the 100 most important albums of all time by *Time* magazine

1974: *Jolene* The song "Jolene" was her second #1 song

1977: *Here You Come Again* First album to go platinum (selling more than a million copies)

1974: *Love Is Like a Butterfly* Title song opened every episode of her TV show

1976: *All I Can Do* Earned Dolly a Grammy nomination

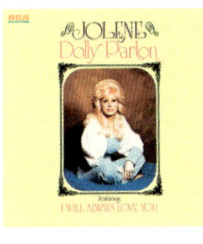

Jolene
In addition to the title song, this album contained the #1 hit "I Will Always Love You." Dolly has said she wrote both songs in the same night.

1975: *The Bargain Store* Title song became Dolly's sixth #1 hit

1977: *New Harvest...First Gathering* Title song hit country charts at #1 and pop charts at #71

FIRST LADIES OF COUNTRY: Rose Maddox (1925–1998)
Rose Maddox and her brothers started a bluegrass band when she was just 11 years old. Their style was a mixture of folk music, swing, jazz, old-time country, gospel, and boogie-woogie. It helped define the sound of an era. Rose paved the way for many future artists, including Dolly.

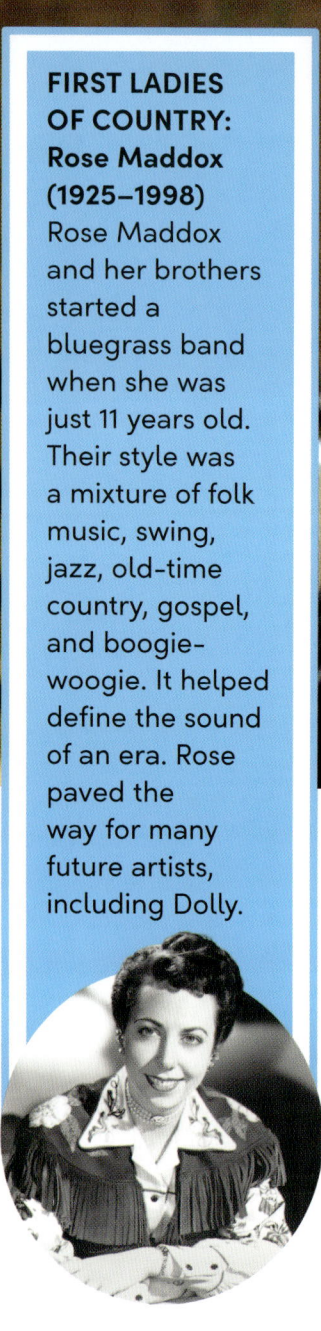

Dolly wrapped up the 1970s with more hits under her rhinestone belt. She'd proved that she appealed to fans of different styles of music. Her final two albums of the decade tiptoed into a new music category: rock. Fans loved it!

Dolly performing on *The Russell Harty Show*, 1977

Dolly was 35. She'd conquered radio, TV, and the Billboard charts. What would she do next? Dolly packed her bags, said goodbye to the Tennessee hills, and headed for Hollywood.

Jane Fonda, Lily Tomlin, Dolly Parton, and Dabney Coleman in *9 to 5*

THE SCREEN COMES CALLING

When Dolly goes after something, she never does it in a small way. Her first-ever movie, 1980's *9 to 5*, earned her three Golden Globe nominations, two Grammys, a People's Choice Award, and an Oscar nomination for Best Song.

Dolly, Jane Fonda, and Lily Tomlin in a scene from the movie

9 to 5 was groundbreaking for its time. It was about three women in the workplace who team up to take down their badly behaving boss. The movie shed a light on the different ways men and women were treated at work. In the movie's title song, Dolly's lyrics make a point about this unfairness.

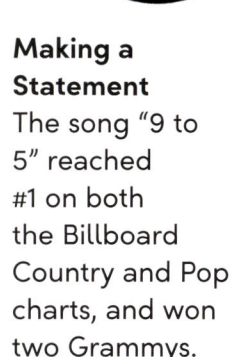

Making a Statement
The song "9 to 5" reached #1 on both the Billboard Country and Pop charts, and won two Grammys.

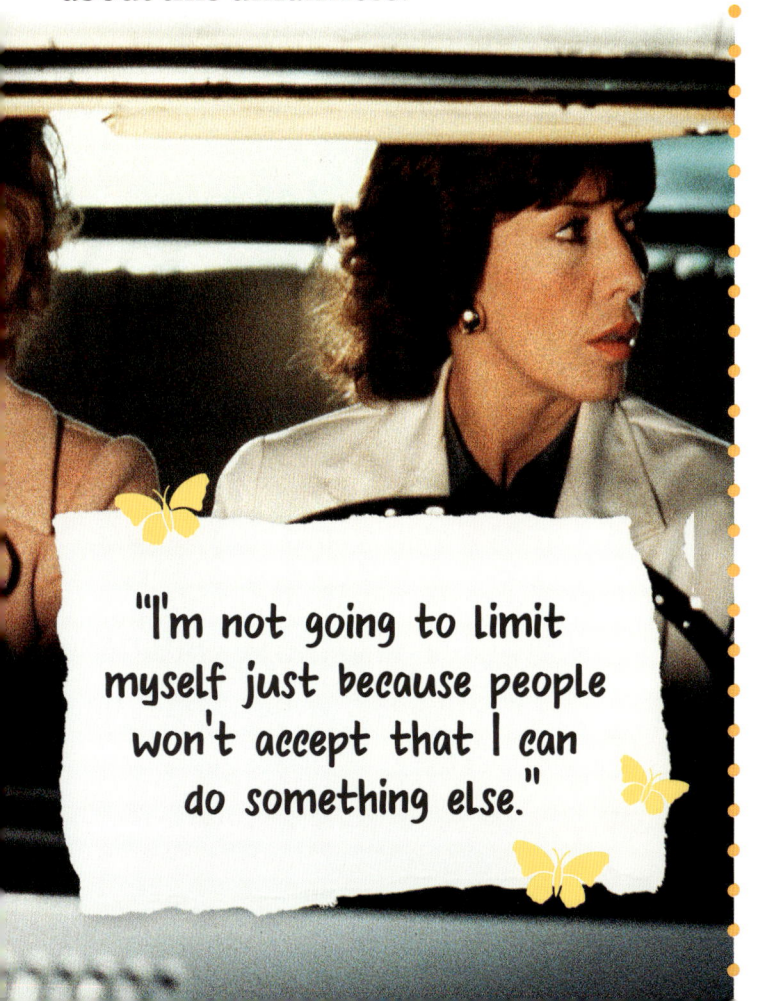

"I'm not going to limit myself just because people won't accept that I can do something else."

Dolly and co-star Sylvester Stallone, 1984

Dolly starred in another popular film in 1982, earning another Grammy for the featured song "Hard Candy Christmas." But her next movie, *Rhinestone* (1984), got terrible reviews, even joking nominations for "Worst Picture of the Year." However, her co-star, Sylvester Stallone, looks fondly back on working with Dolly. He's called it "the best time" he's ever had.

As usual, Dolly didn't give up. In 1989, she starred in *Steel Magnolias*, which earned her co-star Julia Roberts an Oscar nomination. Since then, she's appeared in more than 20 more films.

The Power of the Pen
Dolly has written songs for Whitney Houston, Tina Turner, Jennifer Nettles, Merle Haggard, Kenny Rogers, Emmylou Harris, Queen Latifah, and Miley Cyrus. She has said, "I can write *any* kind of music, any style." She's written gospel, country, bluegrass, R&B, rock, pop, and more.

As her film career rolled on, Dolly never ignored her first love, music. In 1986, she was invited to join the Nashville Songwriters Hall of Fame. Dolly has always loved sharing her words with the world, even if she wasn't the one to sing them. She has written over 3,000 songs, and 450 of them have been recorded.

Emmylou Harris

Dolly and Kenny Rogers

Tina Turner

Queen Latifah

FIRST LADIES OF COUNTRY: Patsy Cline (1932–1963)

Patsy Cline was the most successful country artist of her day and the first woman to be elected into the Country Music Hall of Fame. She was also the first person to ask to be admitted to the Grand Ole Opry, rather than waiting for an invitation. Sadly, she died in a plane crash at the age of 30, but she recorded 100 songs in her short career.

FROM HOLLYWOOD TO DOLLYWOOD

Dolly's next move was a bit unexpected, and it would change thousands of lives for the better! In 1986, just 10 miles down the road from the tiny one-bedroom cabin where she grew up, Dolly opened her own theme park.

When Dolly was a little girl, she loved when the carnival came to town. She dreamed that if she ever became rich and famous, she'd open a "mountain Disneyland." As soon as she could, Dolly bought an old amusement park and gave it a makeover. Welcome to Dollywood!

Don't Wig Out!
Dolly Parton has never ridden any of the fast rides at Dollywood. She gives two reasons why: she gets motion sickness, and she doesn't want her wig to fly off.

Dollywood pays respect to the traditions and history of the area, serving up southern food and themed attractions. It also has live musical performances and personal touches around every corner. Some of Dolly's brothers and sisters used to perform around the park!

More Pie Please! The award-winning food at Dollywood is based on recipes from Dolly's momma's own kitchen. If you're hungry, try the 25-pound apple pie. Just one slice feeds four adults!

Do the Locomotion
One of the more popular attractions is the Dollywood Express, two trains that travel five miles (8 km) around the outside of the park. But they're more than a ride—they're a piece of history. The steam engines were used to deliver supplies during World War II.

Dolly's goal in building her dream park was to "provide jobs for the local people, my family, my neighbors, and my friends to help the local community." The first year the park opened as Dollywood, attendance tripled—and it's still going strong today. More than a million people visit the park each year.

The area around Sevierville and Pigeon Forge has blossomed, with dozens of new museums, shops, restaurants, and more. Dolly added a water park and a dinner show. Today, the park has thousands of employees. And it's brought tens of thousands more jobs to the surrounding area.

In a Jam
On opening day in 1986, so many people tried to visit the park it created a huge traffic jam. Rows of cars were backed up on the interstate for six miles (9.7 km)!

**Go with
Your Gut**
That song Dolly didn't want to sell to Elvis? Holding out paid off! When Whitney Houston rerecorded "I Will Always Love You," Dolly said she made enough money that she could have bought Graceland, Elvis's famous mansion.

TAKING CARE OF BUSINESS

Dolly continued to make music into the next decade. In 1991, the album *Eagle When She Flies* produced another #1 hit, "Rockin' Years." Dolly became the first woman to have a #1 country hit in three different decades.

In 1993, Dolly recorded the album *Honky Tonk Angels* with Loretta Lynn and Tammy Wynette. It paid respect to women who had come before them, including Kitty Wells and Patsy Cline.

Loretta Lynn, Dolly Parton, and Tammy Wynette, 1993

The same year, Whitney Houston recorded Dolly's "I Will Always Love You" for the movie *The Bodyguard*, sending it to the top of the charts once again.

Whitney Houston

FIRST LADIES OF COUNTRY: Tammy Wynette (1942–1998) Tammy Wynette is known for giving women a voice in a genre dominated by men. She communicated emotion through song in a unique way. Her heartache-filled songs reflected a tough personal life many people could identify with.

Good Reads
Dolly's first book was #1 on the *New York Times* bestseller list for two months. She has since written many other books, including cookbooks, children's books, and fiction!

By 1994, Dolly had a lot to talk about, so she put it in a book! Her autobiography, *Dolly: My Life and Other Unfinished Business*, was an instant bestseller. The book talked about crossing over to different genres. She said "old-timers" complained she was leaving country music, but Dolly said it was simply "taking her to new places."

Dolly signing copies of her children's book *I Am a Rainbow*

Multitalented
Most people know Dolly Parton for her voice, but she's a talented instrumentalist as well. In fact, she plays 20 instruments, including the dulcimer, saxophone, hand flute, autoharp, banjo, mandolin, and penny whistle!

One of those places was back to her roots. Dolly grew up listening to bluegrass. With its twangy banjo and fast harmonies, would a bluegrass album be as good as her others? In 1999, *The Grass Is Blue* won the Grammy for best bluegrass album.

Dolly in 2005

Record-Breakers

Dolly Parton has broken 10 Guinness World Records, including:

- Longest Span of #1 Hits on the US Hot Country Songs chart
- Most Studio Albums Released by a Female Country Singer
- First Country Singer to be Nominated for an Emmy, Grammy, Oscar, and Tony

"I don't work for those awards... But that's a nice compliment for people to think that I might deserve it."

Dolly Parton's mark on the world was highlighted in the early 2000s, when she was recognized with some of the highest honors an artist can receive. She was named a Living Legend by the Library of Congress in 2004. This honor paid tribute to the contributions she had made to culture and music history.

In 2005, she won the National Medal of the Arts. This award is the highest honor that can be given to someone in the arts by the government of the United States.

Bright Lights, Big City

A stage version of Dolly's 1980 movie *9 to 5* debuted on Broadway in April of 2009. Dolly wrote all the music and lyrics, which earned her a Tony Award nomination.

Cast of the Broadway musical *9 to 5*

In 2007, Dolly launched her own record label, Dolly Records. She never wanted to sign other artists. She just wanted complete control over her music. Talent took her to the top. But it's her smart business sense that has kept her there.

Money Matters
Dolly may be one of the wealthiest musicians in the world, but she doesn't act like it! The star lives in an average-size home outside of Nashville. She's said she only needs a "comfy chair" for Carl and a porch swing for the backyard. Her one exception? She splurges on wigs and costumes. All of her custom stage attire is handmade, and each piece costs thousands of dollars!

"I have a pretty good gut... I depend on my own higher wisdom of knowing if I'm in the right place with the right people."

Dolly's wig collection on display at the 2013 CMA Music Festival

By 2010, Dollywood had doubled in size, and it's still expanding today. Dolly has also launched other businesses—from pet supplies to cake mixes, spas, perfume, and more. But the work she's most passionate about is giving back to the community that raised her.

Keeping Promises
Dolly started the Imagination Library as a promise to her father. Robert grew up working on a farm, and he never learned to read or write, though Dolly has said he was the smartest man she ever knew. She promised him she would do her best to make sure every child would have access to books.

GIVING FROM THE HEART

Dolly first started the Dollywood Foundation in 1988 to help children with their education. In the early 1990s, Dolly promised to give every seventh and eighth grader in Sevier County $500 if they graduated from high school. The graduation rate increased from 65 percent to 94 percent!

In 1995, she started Dolly Parton's Imagination Library. The program gets children up to age five excited about reading by sending them a free book each month. At first, this was a local program. Then it spread nationwide, and now Dolly sends books to kids in five different countries. To date, Dolly has gifted more than 250 million books!

Dolly reading from her children's book *Coat of Many Colors* at the Library of Congress, 2018

"If you see someone without a smile today, give 'em yours."

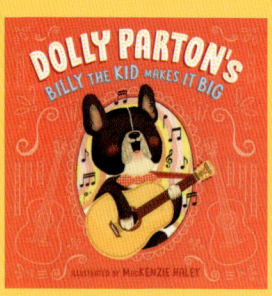

Billy the Kid
Dolly has been a dog owner all her life. These days, she's often seen in the company of a French bulldog named Billy the Kid. In fact, she created a line of picture books about him! He actually belongs to her manager, but she calls him her "god-dog."

Dolly is also passionate about animal welfare. Dollywood is home to the Eagle Mountain Sanctuary, a rescue home for bald eagles unable to be released into the wild due to injury. Visitors to the park can see the majestic birds in their 30,000-square-foot enclosure.

She is also a dog lover. In 2022, she launched a line of pet clothing, toys, and products called Doggy Parton. It includes all your pup could want, from T-shirts to tennis balls. A portion of the company's profit goes to support a local Tennessee farm rescue.

No Pawtographs, Please!
In 2024, Dolly hosted a star-studded TV special called *Dolly Parton's Pet Gala*. It featured country acts, but the main focus was a fashion show for dogs.

Dolly with school kids during an Imagination Library event in the UK in 2007

Over the course of Dolly's career, she has hosted many hospital benefits and donated to medical causes, such as researching cures for childhood cancer. Her foundation sponsors countless scholarships. She's come to the aid of families who've been affected by wildfires and floods. In 2020, during the COVID-19 pandemic, she donated a million dollars toward coronavirus research, helping to develop life-saving vaccines.

In 2022, Dolly received the Carnegie Medal of Philanthropy. This award honors people who make significant contributions to a cause. Upon receiving the award, she said she just "gives from the heart."

"I think it probably was [God's] plan for me not to have kids so everybody's kids could be mine. And they are now."

A Mother to Many

In 1984, she was diagnosed with a medical condition that required surgery. Partially due to this, she never had children of her own. Instead, she focused her work on benefitting children and her community. And she considers herself a "mom" to many, including many nieces and nephews. Her goddaughter, singer Miley Cyrus, calls her "Aunt Dolly."

When Dolly was 15, her parents sold the one-bedroom cabin she had loved so much. Her mother cried. Dolly said "Don't cry, Momma. I'll buy it back for you when I get rich." She did, and she still owns it to this day.

Her parents died in the early 2000s, but they were proud of her every day of her life. Her dad used to sneak out at night to secretly clean the statue of her that sat outside the city courthouse.

Today, Dolly is as busy as ever. In 2023, she released a rock album. She often makes TV appearances. She was a musical guest at the 2023 Thanksgiving Day NFL halftime show.

When she's not busy being the life of the party, she enjoys a quieter life with her husband Carl and sometimes her god-dog, Billy the Kid.

What's next for Dolly? "I have new dreams every day," she's said. "You have to get out there, make those dreams come true."

"Find out who you are and do it on purpose."

GLOSSARY

Album
A collection of songs released by an artist

Autobiography
An account of a person's life written by that person

Charts
A ranking system for popular songs, based on album sales, downloads, and how often songs are played on the radio or streamed on music apps

Duet
A musical performance by two people

Dulcimer
A stringed musical instrument popular in the Appalachian Mountains

Encore
A continuation of a performance called for by audience applause

Immigrant
A person who leaves one country to live permanently in a new country

Mandolin
A musical instrument with metal strings that looks like a small guitar

Memento
An object that reminds you of a time or place

Penny whistle
A whistle made of tin, commonly a children's toy

Philanthropy
Giving of oneself or one's resources to benefit others

Potential
The chance to become or do something

Publishing rights
Legal ownership of a written song or text

Record label
A company that manufactures, promotes, and distributes an artist's music

Sharecropper
A farmer who farms on rented farmland in exchange for sharing the crops with the landowner

Stereotype
A belief about a group or category of people based on prejudiced ideas or assumptions

Venue
A place for performance

Welfare
The state of doing well

INDEX

QUIZ

Answer the questions to see what you have learned. Check your answers in the key below.

1. What was the name of Dolly's first guitar?

2. What is the highest honor that can be given to someone in the arts by the US government?

3. What is the name of Dolly's god-dog?

4. True or False: Dolly Parton has broken 10 Guinness World Records.

5. Which star helped Dolly launch her career by having her as his duet partner on his show?

1. Baby Martin 2. National Medal of the Arts 3. Billy the Kid
4. True 5. Porter Wagoner